DELIVERANCE FROM MIND CONTROL:

BE FREE AND DELIVERED FROM EVERY MARINE DEMONS OF MIND CONTROL

JOHANNES TEFO

Deliverance From Mind Control: Be Free And Delivered From Every Marine Demons Of Mind Control

Johannes Tefo

Published by Johannes Tefo, 2024.

Also by Johannes Tefo

Family spiritual Warfare Books
Youth's Guide To Spiritual Warfare
A Women's Guide To Spiritual Warfare

Standalone
Deliver Your Soul From Evil
Overcoming Spirit Of Stagnation
The 24: Prophetic Word For This Season 2024 And Beyond
Michael For Warfare
Territorial Spirits: Overcome Evil Strongholds in Your Life And
Take Over Your Community With Strategic Warfare And
Winning Prayers
Prayers Against Suicide Spirit
Spiritual Warfare When Enough is Enough
Identity In Christ
Prayers Against Satanic Networks
The Workplace You Need: Spiritual Warfare Prayers That
Silence Evil Powers At Your Workplace.

Deliverance From Mind Control: Be Free And Delivered From Every Marine Demons Of Mind Control

Table of Contents

I dedicate this work to the beleivers all over the mind.
Be delivered in the name of Jesus!

Introduction

A healthy mind is healthy living. You are blessed with the most important assets ever—mind. Your mind, emotions, and feelings make up your personality and soul. Since the foundation of the world, God has given man free will. A free will to choose between blessing or curse. A free will to choose between life and death. You will often hear conspiracies that this and that has sold their soul to the other side.

The enemy has always wanted to pull strings in our minds. He has always wanted to control our minds. Your mind is the greatest asset you have on this planet. A defeated mind cannot operate at its full potential. A mind covered by the blood of the Lamb is capable of much more. All man ought to have the mind of Christ.

The creative power of your mind is a remarkable gift attributed to the divine. It is a force that has shaped our world, driving innovation, artistry, and progress throughout history. And the enemy wants to rob many freedom in the Lord—filling many with unfruitful thoughts of condemnation and low self-esteem.

Here are nine things your mind is capable of:

Imagination: Your mind has the remarkable ability to conjure up ideas, images, and concepts that have never before existed. This power of imagination enables you to envision new possibilities and groundbreaking ideas for changing this world into a better place.

Innovation: Creativity is at the heart of innovation. It is through creative thinking that you develop new technologies, solve complex problems, and improve your quality of life. From the invention of the wheel to the development of modern medicine, human creativity has driven progress throughout the ages.

Artistic Expression: The arts are a testament to the creative power of the human mind. Through painting, music, literature, and other forms of expression, you can convey complex emotions, tell stories, and capture the beauty of the human experience. Art transcends boundaries. And it comes straight out of your God-given brain.

Problem Solving: Creativity is essential for solving everyday challenges and global crises alike. Whether it's finding new ways to address climate change or devising innovative solutions to personal problems, creative minds have the potential to revolutionize the world.

Adaptability: Our ability to adapt and evolve is closely tied to our creative faculties. When faced with new circumstances or obstacles, we can draw on our creativity to develop novel strategies and approaches.

Connection to Spirituality: This is the most important of all, creativity is a spiritual gift, a way to connect with the spirit of Almighty God. You are to love God with all your heart, soul, spirit, and might. The soul itself encompasses of will, emotions, and feelings, and these make up your personality.

Collaboration: The creative power of the human mind becomes even more potent when combined with the creative minds of others. Collaboration and the exchange of ideas often lead to groundbreaking innovations and artistic endeavors that transcend the abilities of any single individual.

Positive Change: Throughout history, creative individuals and movements have been at the forefront of positive change. From civil rights leaders who envisioned a more just society to scientists who work to cure diseases, creative thinking has driven progress and shaped a better future.

Personal Fulfillment: Engaging in creative pursuits can bring a deep sense of fulfillment and purpose. It allows us to tap into our unique talents and passions, leading to a more enriched and meaningful life.

The mind is the greatest asset given to us to continue the work of creation here on earth. Therefore, the changing of your situation begins in the mind. However, the greatest battlefield in man's life is the mind.

The mind is the reasoning faculty of man; it is the center of the decision or intellect of a person. It is the entry point into a person's life. Battles are either won or lost, in the mind; the mind can be easily accessed by the devil. This is why the Word of God warns: *"Keep thy heart with all diligence; for out of it are the issues of life"* (**Proverbs 4:23**).

As human beings, we have a tripartite nature – spirit, soul, and body. Our soul has three realms – the mind, the will, and the emotion. For a person to be sound, his/her triune

1 Thessalonians 5:23 says: *"And the very God of peace sanctify you wholly; and I pray God your whole spirit and soul and body be preserved blameless unto the coming of our Lord Jesus Christ."*

After I stopped going to a certain church, having had revelations from God that the bishop of the church was in the cult, I started experiencing traumatic experiences in my mind. At times, I felt like going crazy. I will hear voices in my mind and in my sleep. The spirit of confusion and madness was after me. And the spirit of death. I spent the whole three years attacked in my dreams, and having uncontrollable out-of-body experiences—going to strange places that I can't even explain.

It daunts me that the bishop of the church cursed me for leaving the church. it is common in African-initiated churches for men of God to curse their members if they threaten to leave the church. I wouldn't even call it a church but a cult.

Many can attest to what I am saying, especially African brothers and sisters in various denominations, it comes with strange spiritual attacks when leaving these African-initiated churches since they will make you feel that their church is the only church capable of deliverance. Many churches I have seen, work with different powers from the kingdom of darkness. Especially many churches that make selling healing and deliverance products their focal point. They all come from the marine kingdom.

Don't get me wrong, not all churches that use water come from the marine world but the majority of them. Many times I was rebuked by the Lord for making healing objects the focal point of my faith. It is the Word that heals. It is the Word and spirit of Christ that make a difference in all things—especially in deliverance and healing.

And I have come to the conclusion that many believers who struggle with marine powers have gone to these kinds of churches for help. Or rather, went to traditional doctors for spiritual healing and other things. A man or woman will do anything for his or her health.

It took me a long toll to dismantle the marine forces and powers of darkness in my life. It is not a child's play to deal with powers from the water realm. Because water is life and you literally use water for everyday needs and everyday living. It was once revealed to me that kings and queens in our soil if they wanted power to control or rule the town or village, would go to rivers and streams where many fetch water there to curse the water—speaking incantations over water that everyone drinking from that stream shall be subjected unto them.

It is the same when one partakes in water rituals, candle rituals, and others I would not mention. You will be subjected unto gods that you do not know. Many perish because of a lack of knowledge. In these last days, Satan no longer hides in the dark like he used to. Now he prowls freely in our playground.

And he has always wanted to control and influence the minds of people. If you are not in Christ, you will fall prey because it is the Holy Spirit of God that defends us against the millions of wiles of this entity. Ancient civilization had fought with this entity, and we are also to wage spiritual warfare against him for us to be winners. The term "spiritual warfare" is not a light term. It is the real spiritual fight between the children of light and the children of darkness. As always light will prevail, but we have to know our way in this battle.

For so long, the church of Christ has been on the defensive side, it is time we march to the battle line and wage warfare—attack as we walk in high authority and power. When you trust the Most High, a mere you can defend thousands and thousands. The righteous are bold as lions. It is time to step up the game. The enemy is always working behind the scenes to put us to sleep.

The spirit of slumbering and prayerlessness is a spiritual attack from the evil one. I have noticed that our generation is becoming more anti-God and anti-Christ more and more. And I have also observed that there are more evil strongholds that are affecting our society and culture on a larger scale which are, religious spirit, anti-Crist spirit, Octopus spirit (Mind control), gluttony spirit, leviathan spirit (pride), slumbering spirit (Laziness) and spirit of heaviness (Depression).

There are many but these are barriers in the lives of humankind. Remember, Eve's sin was through food. Esau's disobedience to the call of God was through food. In our day and age, pleasure is derived from eating more than anything. Man cannot live by bread alone. Many times we will prepare to consecrate and humble ourselves before Almighty God but food will get in our way to distract us from harkening to the voice of God.

As I already told you I was serving in a church that was a cult, after I left the church I started feeling like the spirit of madness was following me. When you have seen things that you were not supposed to see, they will try by all means necessary to destroy you or kill you. The bishop of the church serves many gods; some I will say are ancient gods that we read about in the bible.

The majority of pagan religions, especially African religions, serves nature, water gods and goddess, mountain gods and goddess, and the underworld spirits, evoking the ancestral spirits for blessings, luck, and protection. King Manasseh of Judah bowed and worshipped the sun, moon, and stars. This is the same practice of many men and women of God who stand on the pulpit preaching to you the message of Christ. I so wish the body of Christ could walk more in the spirit of discernment to see what we are up against. Many prophets, pastors, religious leaders, and preachers are not for us.

They are serving a different Christ we do not know. My African, my land, is covered with an anti-Christ spirit and is moving the anti-Christ movement further and further. African spirituality is the term that makes many feel Enlighted or awakened, by indulging in spirituality tapping into the whole spiritual world governed mainly by fallen creatures. God is above nature. It is the spirit of God that will lead us to the path of righteousness. Other spirits, lead to spiritual destruction.

I found myself battling—ridding water covenants of different snake spirits. Territorial spirits of wickedness also, that blind believers to see the truth. I have also noted that the culture and tradition we are fond of so much were inspired and influenced by demons. It is without a doubt, that in my African soil, the land was covenanted to the demons. There is a long way to go. I strongly believe that through the blood of the Lamb, we shall conquer.

The Lord revealed to me the spirit of mind control that is gripping many. And I was also the victim—and that is octopus spirit. There are the marine spirit demons that cover the heads of many to never receive the gospel of Jesus. Marine agents put this spirit on your head. And they can also affect the whole village or town by covering it with this squid spirit of mind control.

Through this spirit, they are able to control your mind and influence you to do things against your will. Besides control and influence, this spirit inflicts pain such as headaches, migraines, and overall pain over your head. You will feel a deep pain as if someone is pressing it on your head. Some headaches are abnormal. There is a normal headache and an abnormal one.

My whole family lineage has been struggling with headaches. A week would not pass by without someone falling sick. It has become a stronghold. The Holy Spirit of God reveals all truth. If it was not the spirit of God, I would not have known some of the generational spirits that have been within my family bloodline.

I strongly believe that idol worship and rebellion is the stronghold of many families around the world. And many want a way out through their own power and might. Sadly, it does not happen that way. Only salvation comes from the Lord.

Psalm 3:8 Salvation belongeth unto the LORD: thy blessing is upon thy people. Selah.

Redemption of God is permanent. By His mighty Hand, He has delivered the children of Israel of out the house of bondage. Egypt in the realm of spirit is bondage. You also might be in bondage facing backlash and spiritual attacks from the house of your forefathers, know that the strong arm of the Lord is able to rid you of bondage.

Like a mighty warrior, God has delivered His chosen from the land of Ham. He will also do the same if you keep the faith and never back down. Trust in the Lord and in His salvation. Salvation of God is through the blood of Jesus Christ that brings all nations, languages, and people to the very house of God.

What is Octopus Spirit?

An Octopus spirit is a ruling spirit that is operating in conjunction with various tentacles, which are demonic spirits and sins of the flesh. The head is typically a spirit of idolatry or witchcraft (control). It is a marine demon used by the agents of Lucifer to manipulate and control the mind of people, both believers and non-believers can be victims.

Bear in mind, that this spirit can affect people individually and territorially. A nation can be hit with an octopus's spirit and be blinded from accepting the gospel of Jesus Christ.

In whom the god of this world hath blinded the minds of them which believe not, lest the light of the glorious gospel of Christ, who is the image of God, should shine unto them. (II Corinthians 4:4)

Satan uses your own mouth, your eyes, ears, and even your senses of touch and smell to foster wicked thoughts in your mind.

BLINDING MINDS OF UNBELIEVERS: Satan works in the minds of unbelievers to blind them to the truth of the Gospel:

Believers ought to renew their minds through the help of the Holy Spirit. we are wrestling with evil unseen forces in high places that never get tired. Spirits never get tired. They work patiently and diligently till they accomplish their evil purpose in the life of believers. It is vital that we never open doors for these kinds of spirits. It is an intense deliverance process of the mind. Guard your spirit, soul, and body at all times. Let God be the center of your pleasure and joy.

I personally know the pain of dealing with mind-controlling spirits. The octopus directs the arms for the purpose of grabbing, holding, and constraining the prey from moving forward. The arms also have a bit of autonomy to operate apart from the head and can grow back if they are cut off. In the same way, people who are being tormented and controlled by the octopus' spirit may get deliverance from one fleshly demon only to find the same or similar snare sneaking back up on them during a more 'opportune time.'

Octopuses are super smart and adept at finding their way into tiny places both to hide from predators and to go after their prey. They can change the shape of their bodies and fit into the tiniest of places.

A person may not know that they are still dealing with these demons once they have experienced liberation, because they will keep to themselves when they are about to be discovered. Octopuses are experts in the art of camouflage to avoid predators. They can blend in with their surroundings by changing shape and color.

This spirit manifests itself in the life of a believer by persuading him to engage in ungodly sexual relationships, which are presented as a sacred union. Another attack is to deceive a person into believing that their situation is different in a way that means particular Bible verses do not apply to them.

I have known people who, under the influence of the Octopus spirit, brazenly declared that God had told them that someone else's husband would be their husband, others who said that God had ordained their marriage. having sex with an illegitimate lover by marrying them into heaven, and another believing that Jesus was helping them to masturbate in a holy way to avoid falling into a sexual relationship with another person. All of these people are slaves to lustful desires and are under the control of the octopus spirit.

You, my brothers and sisters, were called to be free. But do not use your freedom to indulge the flesh; rather, serve one another humbly in love. For the entire law is fulfilled in keeping this one command: "Love your neighbor as yourself." If you bite and devour each other, watch out or you will be destroyed by each other.

• • • •

"**THEREFORE** I say, walk **in** the Spirit, and you will not gratify the desires of the flesh.

For the flesh desires what is contrary to the Spirit, and the Spirit **desires** what is contrary to the flesh.

They **contradict** each other so you **shouldn't** do **what** you want.

But if you are led by the Spirit, you are not under the law.

"**The deeds** of the flesh are **evident:**

fornication, impurity and debauchery; idolatry and witchcraft; hatred, discord, jealousy, **anger,** selfish ambition, **discord, faction** and envy; drunkenness, **etc.**

I warn you, as I **have warned you** before, that those who live like this will not inherit the kingdom of God.

Galatians 5:13-25

For those who have been freed from carnal addictions such as pornography, gluttony, rage, jealousy, and selfish ambition, this group of demons will wait for the moment when the person will be weakened by the pressure force of life or when it regularly neglects spiritual disciplines. pray, study, fast, and try to get through every crack they can find.

For example, a married person who was once addicted to pornography, if they are not careful to love, pursue, and cherish their partner, may find that they constantly notice and think about co-workers or have negative reactions. romantic or sexual response to other women... It is not enough to simply do evil, we must also let ourselves be guided by the Holy Spirit to do good.

Octopus spirits are a group of spirits gifted with witchcraft, sometimes in the form of controlling or Jezebel spirits, or idolaters, as leaders, and the spirits are named after mortal sins their respective flesh as lust, anger, selfish ambition or gluttony. arm. To gain and maintain freedom, we must stop cutting off hands and attacking the head.

Surrendering complete and total control of your life to the Lordship of Jesus Christ is the only way to **be** free from **black magic** or **mind control** and **serve only** God and **put** Him first in **everything Work** is the only way to **liberate yourself** and stay **free of** idolatry.

Attacking the head and arms will **result in death.**

Cut off the **arm** and leave the head intact and the **arm** will grow back, the demon will go **and make someone else** more evil than **it was,** and **eventually, that person's** condition will **become** worse than **at the beginning.**

The effect of Octopus spirit

This mind applies mental and physical pressure. When the soul does this to the host, the host will do the same to others. The person will try to confuse someone, etc. This demon persuades people to engage in immoral sexual relations, orgies, pornography, masturbation, and lascivious desires and takes natural desires and distorts them. This spirit encourages people to satisfy lustful needs beyond what God commands. People who operate in this spirit exhibit addictive behavior, obsessive patterns, rage, and excessive food cravings (gluttony), and they attempt to exhibit ungodly relationships as a combination. sacred. For example, homosexuality, same-sex marriage, sleeping with married people and claiming to be husband and wife, swinging, etc. There are also acts of rape and sabotage.

The spirit and the flesh are always in conflict with each other. The habitual sin of the flesh is an open door. This mind can manifest as unusual headaches, migraines, nightmares, blocked dreams, psychosis, pressure in the back or front of the head, blurred or distorted vision, difficulty breathing, suffocation or feeling of suffocation, patterns, and cycles recur, and this ruler bends and twists one's will and flesh. You may start to notice distortions in people who have been busy for a while. This ruler's dominance can also cause brain and mental disorders.

It is apparent that one has to be intentional about being delivered and staying delivered. This ruler will not be cast out by religious prayers. This demonic spirit is very strong. You have to know what you are contending with. The demon spoke to the gentleman who was excited about casting out devils, but that devil said Peter and Paul I know but who are you. Jesus, I know but who are you. It will take spiritual authority and deep faith to cast this out. The apostles could not free the possessed boy but only Jesus could.

The octopus' purpose is to dismantle ministries from within. It can be prayer, preaching, etc. It is a spirit to overthrow. There has to be temperance in all things. If one is delivered from a tentacle or an arm, that spirit can regenerate and come back. The octopus must be decapitated. The head is idolatry, witchcraft, and control. Remember the main tactic is perversion.

Before you are born again your spirit is dead to God. (Genesis 2:17). After you are born again, your spirit comes alive to God and the Holy Spirit lives in you. A battle begins between your soul and your spirit. Satan works against your soul to keep you from progressing spiritually. Satan wants to keep you an immature, carnal Christian, unable to live by the Holy Spirit.

The soul is the mind, emotions, and will. The mind decides what the body will do and then sends instructions to the body. For example, if you are going to walk, your mind tells your legs to move. If you are to talk, your mind tells you to open your mouth and what to speak.

When mind-control demons are present, they fight your spirit at every turn. It becomes very difficult to obey God, even though you want to. Joyce Meyers said that the Battlefield is in the mind. Mind control is the chief weapon of Satan to trap you and keep him in bondage:

Lest Satan should take advantage of us, for we are not ignorant of his devices (traps). 2 Corinthians 2:11

Demons attack our minds because from there they are in a strong position to affect every area of our life.

We are surely dealing with principalities and powers of darkness. I remember at one time in my life as I was going through spiritual attacks, I was praying, and fasting, basically doing what I know that could save me. One night I had a dream where I saw Apostle Paul giving me this scripture;

Ephesians 6:12 For we wrestle not against flesh and blood, but against principalities, against powers, against the rulers of the darkness of this world, against spiritual wickedness in high places.

It is still a mystery to people who were dealing with spiritual wickedness in high places. The high place is a realm over the highest mountains where evil spirits are hovering around with evil influences over the regions. The goal of every demon is to find a body to dwell in. and they will always find a way in through disobedience of the Word of God. Demons oppress both believers and non-believers alike.

While Christ was on earth, he delivered both those who were believers and those who weren't. a young girl who was crippled by the spirit of infirmity was a daughter of Abraham. She must have been a believer since she was called the daughter of Abraham. Even in the body of Christ, we see believers in the bondage of ancestral ties, familiar spirits, and demonic powers of evil retraining them from fulfilling the call of God.

It is a silly debate and discussion whether a demon can be in a believer's life or not. Many theologies deny that a believer in Christ can have a demon. As long as we are living in this cold world of evil, man will always struggle with the forces of evil, some will prevail and some will not. In the last days, even the elect will be deceived. Deception is a spiritual manipulation.

The war started in heaven. You will often wonder why Lucifer was able to influence millions of angels to reject their Maker to follow him. It is still a mystery. As human beings, we are no match to fallen spirits. It is by the grace of the Most High that we can proudly say "We are more than conquerors". It is the spirit of God that lives in you that is mightier.

. . . .

SATAN'S KINGDOM:

Demons are set up in a hierarchy, like an army – Commander down to foot soldiers. The more powerful demons are at a higher rank. Weaker demons are at a lower rank and answer to the higher-rank demons. Demons hate each other but are trained to work together to afflict man. When under attack (in deliverance) demons will work together to keep from being cast out. The strongest demons are Mind-Control demons. This is why Paul told us:

For though we walk in the flesh, we do not war against the flesh. For the weapons of our warfare are not carnal but mighty in God for pulling down strongholds, casting down arguments and every high thing that exalts itself against the knowledge of God, bringing every thought into captivity to the obedience of Christ. 2 Corinthians 10:3-5.

When Paul wrote about the principalities and powers of darkness, he talked about the wickedness that is done in the spirit realm located in the second heaven. This is the stronghold of the kingdom of the Devil. You will recall a time when Angel Gabriel was held hostage by the Persian principality, this happened in the spirit realm we cannot see with the naked eye.

These strongmen who are regional in their territory, assigned demons to influence and lead nations astray from God's commands. Mind control is the number one weapon used to influence and harden the hearts of people to never see the truth and accept it. The truth of the gospel of Jesus Christ.

That's why as Christians we have to cover our minds with the blood of Jesus Christ. This is where the blood becomes the potent weapon of warfare. The blood of Jesus brings light and salvation.

For the weapons of our warfare are not carnal but mighty in God for pulling down strongholds, casting down arguments and every high thing that exalts itself against the knowledge of God

When you cast down these mind-controlling demons, in the spirit realm they are falling. Mostly these spirits affect how you think, perceive, and reason. You cannot fully function to your potential while in bondage to the evil powers of the mind. Occult mind control is another serious issue that is destroying the lives of many—especially celebrities and high-ranking people in positions of honor. It is no longer a secret that many bargained with the god of this world to get where they are. Some honor, fame, riches, and power do not come from God but from the Devil.

I saw in a vision a room located in Nigeria that looked like a control room filled with TV screens and people at work looking at the screen, looking at the life of people on earth, this place was underground, and it clicked to me that this is the place where they control their victim.

In the marine kingdom, under the sea, I have also seen a big screen showcasing every place in this world. Marine agents assign demons to believers who are lukewarm and also assign demons from time to time to those who are strong to weaken them and abort their destiny. Marine demons are most of the cruel demons that are stubborn. These demons feed on sex, they usually manipulate their victim through dreams.

It is vital to cover your household with the power of the blood of the lamb. Believers from time to time, should engage in territorial warfare in their communities. Binding and loosing.

The power of God is in your mouth and in the Word of God. You will never go wrong by confessing and proclaiming the Word of God over your family, your life, and your community.

Overthrow the mind-controlling spirit by pleading the blood of the lamb over the atmosphere of your village because the seat of authority of the prince and princess of darkness is in the atmosphere. That's where they launch their attack on you and over your home. The light of God shall cover your home. And angelic activities shall be normal.

Because some land has been sold or covenanted to the Devil. We have to claim our land back and assign everything under the authority of the Holy Spirit. man has authority on Earth and over the sky where planes fly. And also, over the seas, man has authority.

Psalm 8:6 Thou madest him to have dominion over the works of thy hands; thou hast put all things under his feet: 7 All sheep and oxen, yea, and the beasts of the field; 8 The fowl of the air, and the fish of the sea, and whatsoever passeth through the paths of the seas. 9 O LORD our Lord, how excellent is thy name in all the earth!

Deliverance of Mind

1. You must be born again – deliverance is for only those who have given their lives to Jesus Christ. Salvation is the first step to deliverance.

2. Your mindset must change: your beliefs or way of thinking determines your behavior and outlook. **Matthew 12:35**, says: *"A good man out of the good treasure of the heart bringeth forth good things: and an evil man out of the evil treasure bringeth forth evil things."* **James 1:21, 22** also says: *"Wherefore lay apart all filthiness and superfluity of naughtiness, and receive with meekness the engrafted word, which is able to save your souls. But be ye doers of the word, and not hearers only, deceiving your own selves."*

    We change our mindset by continuously reading, studying, meditating and applying God's Word on a daily basis to our lives. Proverbs 11:9 says: *"...but through knowledge shall the just be delivered."*

3. You must avoid Negative thoughts by thinking about the scriptures. **Philippians 4:8:** *"Finally, brethren, whatsoever things are true, whatsoever things are honest, whatsoever things are just, whatsoever things are pure, whatsoever things are lovely, whatsoever things are of good report; if there be any virtue, and if there be any praise, think on these things."* God is big, think and act big. **Thoughts plus Actions = Behavior.** What you think is what you become (**Proverbs. 23:7**). So develop scriptural self-talk, what you tell yourself, will influence

the way you feel and behave. **Romans 10:10** *For with the heart man believeth unto righteousness; and with the mouth confession is made unto salvation.*

4. Keep Good Association: Keep the right company with Godly-minded people. Positive attracts positive. 1 **Corinthinas 15:33:** *"Be not deceived: evil communications corrupt good manners."* If your friends are drunks you will remain a drunk and die as a drunk, save yourself, come out of them!

5. Pray aggressively for your deliverance – through aggressive deliverance prayers, we cast down wrong imaginations. **2 Corinthians 10:5** says, *"Casting down imaginations, and every high thing that exalteth itself against the knowledge of God, and bringing into captivity every thought to the obedience of Christ."* Aggressive prayers address the satanic voices that speak to the mind.

Powerful deliverance

Salvation comes from God. And it belongs to God. By the mighty hand, God of Israel delivered his army from Egypt—the house of bondage. It happened again when the captives returned from Babylon—from the land of Chaldeans. Throughout history, deliverance has come from God.

Years ago, Christ became a sacrificial lamb, redeeming, cleansing, justifying, and sanctifying many who believed through the death of the cross. And again, through resurrection, which indicates that our mortal bodies will also be glorified when we have fought till the end of time.

Christian walk is not a part-time job. You carry the cross till you go home. The secret weapon to deliverance has always been holiness. And it is the blood of the lamb that sanctifies believers and sets them apart from the world.

And they overcame him by the blood of the Lamb and by the word of their testimony, and they did not love their lives to the death.

(Revelation 12:11)

The remedy of freedom from mind control starts when you realize that on your own you cannot do it. we need the holy spirit to empower us to defeat powers from the sky. Because these are powers that are influencing nations—people from all walks of life. Life is spiritual. Things happen in the spirit realm before manifesting themselves in the physical world.

Scriptures say Christ was crucified before the foundation of the world. It means he died first in the spirit realm. The physical death of the cross was a physical manifestation of the spiritual reality. He lived a spiritual life in a spiritual state before he incarnated. Man is first a spirit before he becomes the body. The body is the lowest state of a person.

The real person is the spirit person. It is the breath of God. And the Devil is after your soul more than your body. It is in the capacity of the soul that he deals with us since our soul encompasses will, emotions, and the mind. Folks, when he has your mind, the remedy is total submission under the will of God. If you are all out for God, you will be sold out all to Him.

Resists the enemy, he shall flee from you. Resisting in standing on the ground of the faith in God. Not faith in men or in certain doctrines, but faith in the Lord God through Jesus Christ. We overcame by the blood of the lamb.

The blood of the lamb is the power of God to redeem mankind from the hand of the evil one. If they say "There is no way out" the blood of Jesus says "There is a way".

Psalm 3:1-3 Lord, how are they increased that trouble me! many are they that rise up against me. 2 Many there be which say of my soul, There is no help for him in God. Selah. 3 But thou, O LORD, art a shield for me; my glory, and the lifter up of mine head.

When you feel like things are out of your control and feel distant from the Lord, He is closer than you think. In perilous times, God is nearer than any. There was a time when the army besieged Israel during the reign of Jehoshaphat, here is the weapon of praise being put to action for victory:

The story of Jehoshaphat's deliverance from the enemy is found in the Old Testament of the Bible, specifically in 2 Chronicles 20. Jehoshaphat was the king of Judah and reigned during a period when the nation faced threats from its neighboring enemies, particularly the Moabites and the Ammonites, along with some of the Meunites.

Here is a summary of the story:

1. **The Threatening Coalition**: A vast army of Moabites, Ammonites, and Meunites gathered together to make war against Judah. Jehoshaphat was alarmed by this formidable threat and realized that his kingdom was not strong enough to withstand such an attack.

2. **Seeking God's Guidance**: Jehoshaphat turned to God for guidance and called for a fast throughout all Judah. He gathered the people together in Jerusalem at the temple, and they sought the Lord's help.

3. **Jehoshaphat's Prayer**: In front of the assembly, Jehoshaphat prayed to God, acknowledging His sovereignty and past deeds on behalf of the nation. He cried out for help and guidance, recognizing their vulnerability and their dependence on God's intervention.

4. **A Prophet's Message**: While they were praying, a prophet named Jahaziel, son of Zechariah, received a message from the Lord. He assured Jehoshaphat and the people that the battle was not theirs but God's. He told them not to be afraid or discouraged and that they would not need to fight in this battle.

5. **The Worshipful Response**: In response to the prophet's message, Jehoshaphat and the people bowed down and worshiped God. They praised Him for His holiness and acknowledged their trust in Him.

6. **The Battle Plan**: The next morning, Jehoshaphat led his army, but instead of putting the strongest warriors at the front, he placed the choir and musicians singing praises to the Lord. They went out before the army, saying, "Give thanks to the Lord, for his steadfast love endures forever."

7. **God's Deliverance**: As they began to sing and praise, the Lord set an ambush against the enemies' armies. Confusion broke out among the enemy forces, and they started attacking each other. By the time the people of Judah arrived at the scene, they found their enemies defeated, with no need for them to fight.

8. **The Plunder**: Jehoshaphat's army gathered the spoil of the battle, and it took them three days to collect it all

because there was so much. They praised God in the Valley of Beracah, which means "Valley of Blessing," for the great victory.

This story illustrates the power of prayer, trust in God, and the importance of acknowledging His sovereignty. Jehoshaphat and the people of Judah turned to God in their time of need, and He delivered them in a miraculous way, demonstrating that victory comes from the Lord.

This is an inspiring story that teaches us that in times of war or difficult situations, God is our defense, refuge, and our stronghold. Deliverance comes from the Lord.

Redemption

By the blood of Jesus, we are redeemed:

In Him [Jesus] *we have redemption through His blood.*

(Ephesians 1:7)

Christ paid in full. He literally said, "It is finished while on the cross". Through faith and the grace of God, we enter into the covenant of abundant living. There is deliverance from all kinds of sickness and diseases. Jesus Christ went all about doing good, healing all, and delivering all who we possessed and oppressed by evil powers.

Acknowledge your victory through the blood of the lamb. The mystery is in the power of the blood of the lamb. Apply and cover your mind with the blood of Jesus. Sing holy spirit-inspired songs of deliverance. Scriptures say, whatsoever that is pure, holy or honorable, think of those.

God has not given us the spirit of fear but of power, love, and a sound mind. God wants your sober mind. It is through meditating on the scripture and lifestyle of prayer that we will live a victorious life in our mind. Mindset is the biggest thing the demons go after. A defeated mind cannot lift a finger. It is vital that we guard against what we watch, what we hear, and what we allow in our lives in general.

Psalm 1:2-3 But his delight is in the law of the LORD; and in his law doth he meditate day and night. 3 And he shall be like a tree planted by the rivers of water, that bringeth forth his fruit in his season; his leaf also shall not wither; and whatsoever he doeth shall prosper.

I, personally, have seen great breakthroughs in some areas of my life by merely meditating on the scriptures. Prophesying over myself and confessing healing and deliverance scriptures over my situation. The Lord has come through with His healing wings to cover me. He can do the same for you if you are going through a depressed journey.

And you have to be consistence in prayer. The scripture above says "Meditate day and night". There are arrows of evil that fly day and night.

Psalm 91 says "Thou shalt not be afraid for the terror by night; nor for the arrow that flieth by day; Nor for the pestilence that walketh in darkness; nor for the destruction that wasteth at noonday.

Psalm 121:6 The sun shall not smite thee by day, nor the moon by night.

These Psalms, 91 and 121 talk about terror by night and arrows that flies by day. These are the evil powers of the Devil. Satan is the night rider. He doesn't want his plan to be known or seen. He will manipulate your life behind the scene, you will hate everyone around you thinking they are the ones wishing you bad lucks while there is a guy in the background pulling all the string. Life is spiritual folks.

Principalities and powers in the second heaven control demons that are on earth—commanding them to manipulate and deceive. If the Holy Spirit of God is not your portion, you will likely fall prey to their schemes and devices.

It is not also strange when the Psalmist says *The sun shall not smite thee by day, nor the moon by night,* witches, sorcerers, and wizards are well known for programming the sun and moon for evil purposes. Sun and moon worshippers wake up early in the morning from 3 AM TO 5 AM to command the sun for their personal gain. And at times if they want to curse you or wreck your life, they will program your life through the sun, and you will amount to nothing. These people are destiny killers, stealers, and destroyers.

Stars are also used to program the minds. The stars of Orion. I spent the whole year battling with what I will call Schizophrenia, basically hearing voices from time to time. I have written the whole book about this subject called "Demons Behind Schizophrenia and the second one called "Total Healing Schizophrenia" testifying about the goodness of the Lord and deliverance.

Let the redeemed of the Lord say so, whom He has redeemed from the hand of the enemy.

(Psalm 107:2)

Testimony is the weapon I use against the enemy. Speak about how big your God is and how far He has come with you. The testimony of Jesus Christ is the power of the gospel. In fact, the heart of the gospel is the testimony and the prophecy of Christ.

Early Christians and Apostles conquered by testifying about the death and resurrection of Jesus Christ—the son of the Living God. It is still the same gospel of the demonstration of the power of the Word of God. Folks, this is the Word that renews our minds.

Isaiah 26:3-4 Thou wilt keep him in perfect peace, whose mind is stayed on thee: because he trusteth in thee. 4 Trust ye in the LORD forever: for in the LORD JEHOVAH is everlasting strength:

Isaiah 26:12 LORD, thou wilt ordain peace for us: for thou also hast wrought all our

works in us.

Romans 12:2 And be not conformed to this world: but be ye transformed by the

renewing of your mind, that ye may prove what is that good, and acceptable, and

perfect, will of God.

Cleansing

If we walk in the light as He is in the light, we have fellowship one with another, and the blood of Jesus Christ His Son cleanses us from all sin.

(1 John 1:7)

The unapproachable light is the glory of God. Light represents glory, holiness, and truth. When we have fellowship with these three, we are renewed and transformed into the image of Christ. And the blood of Jesus will continue to cleanse us, sanctify us, and transform our thought process.

Adam was created perfect in all senses. The second Adam who was Christ is the restorer of man's domain. I strongly believe that Adam's body was glorified before sin.

Cleansing your mind through the Word of God is a process that involves immersing yourself in Scripture, meditating on its teachings, and allowing it to transform your thoughts and attitudes. Here are some steps you can take to cleanse your mind through the Word of God:

1. **Regular Bible Reading**: Develop a habit of reading the Bible daily. Choose a specific time and place for your reading, and stick to it. You can start with a particular book or passage, or you can follow a reading plan.

2. **Meditation**: Don't rush through your Bible reading. Take time to meditate on the verses you read. Ponder their meaning and how they apply to your life. Consider memorizing key verses that speak to your heart.

3. **Prayer**: Before and after reading the Bible, pray for understanding and wisdom. Ask God to reveal His truth to you through His Word. Prayer is a vital part of the process of cleansing your mind.

4. **Study Tools**: Use study tools like commentaries, concordances, and Bible dictionaries to help you better understand the context and meaning of the Scriptures.

5. **Application**: Apply the teachings of the Bible to your life. Consider how you can live out the principles and values you find in Scripture. This may involve making changes in your behavior, attitudes, or beliefs.

6. **Renew Your Mind**: Romans 12:2 instructs us not to conform to the patterns of this world but to be transformed by the renewing of our minds. The Word of God is a powerful tool for this transformation. As

you fill your mind with God's truth, it will help replace negative and worldly thoughts with godly ones.

7. **Positive Affirmations**: Use Bible verses as positive affirmations. Whenever you face challenges, doubts, or negative thoughts, counter them with Scripture. For example, if you struggle with fear, meditate on passages that speak of God's protection and peace (e.g., Psalm 91).

8. **Community and Accountability**: Share your journey with other believers. Join a Bible study group or find an accountability partner who can encourage and support you in your efforts to cleanse your mind through the Word of God.

9. **Filtering Media and Entertainment**: Be mindful of what you expose your mind to through media and entertainment. Evaluate whether what you consume aligns with biblical values and principles. Avoid content that promotes negative or ungodly thinking.

10. **Gratitude and Worship**: Develop a heart of gratitude and worship. Regularly thank God for His Word and the transformative work it's doing in your life. Worship Him for His goodness and faithfulness.

11. **Patience and Persistence**: Cleansing your mind is a lifelong process. Be patient with yourself and persistent in your pursuit of a renewed mind. God's Word has the power to transform you over time.

Remember that cleansing your mind through the Word of God is not a one-time event but a continuous journey of growth and transformation. It requires dedication, prayer, and a genuine desire to align your thoughts and beliefs with God's truth.

Justification

By the blood of Jesus, we are justified:

Having now been justified by His blood.

(Romans 5:9)

The word justified means "pronounced or treated as righteous." For a Christian, justification is the act of God not only forgiving the believer's sins but imputing to him the righteousness of Christ. The Bible states in several places that justification only comes through faith (e.g., Romans 5:1; Galatians 3:24). Justification is not earned through our own works; rather, we are covered by the righteousness of Jesus Christ (Ephesians 2:8; Titus 3:5). The Christian, being declared righteous, is thus freed from the guilt of sin.

Faith in Jesus Christ and the power of His blood brings deliverance from various mental issues, including anxiety, depression, addiction, and trauma. Jesus is able to bring healing and peace to troubled minds.

Motivational and inspirational speakers would tell you to think positive thoughts if you want a healthy lifestyle. As a man thinks, so is he. The mind is the biggest asset of every individual on this planet.

Being justified by the blood of Christ, not by our self-righteousness, leads us into the path of righteousness and victory. The Bible says "Resists the Devil, He shall flee. Speak the light of God over your mind. Let the light of God penetrate whatever is not under the control of God. In areas of our lives where God is not in total control, we tend to struggle with evil strongholds from the enemy.

Yield to the spirit of God. God is willing and able to deliver our soul, spirit, and body out of the hands of the enemy. Every day when you wake up before you go outside you put on clothes, we also have to put on spiritual clothes always. You do not want to be vulnerable. Demons are thirsty for our temple. Our bodies are the temple of the spirit of God. A man ought to host the holy ghost with their body.

Scripture declaration is the key. proclamation of the goodness of the Lord and thanksgiving. You do not enter into the presence of God and come out with nothing. Enter into His presence with thanksgiving and His court with praise. This is the secret of entering into the presence of the Most High.

Your mind will feel refreshed after prayer. I have also noted that after every prayer and fasting, I feel relieved and refreshed in my mind. And I have actually been delivered from the spirit of Schizophrenia through fasting, praying, meditating on the Word, and worshipping.

In a nutshell, Justification is that gracious and judicial act of God whereby a soul is granted complete absolution from all guilt and a full release from the penalty of sin (Romans 3:23-25). This act of divine grace is wrought by faith in the merits of our Lord and Savior Jesus Christ (Romans 5:1).

· · · ·

SANCTIFICATION

By the blood of Jesus, we are sanctified:

Therefore Jesus also, that He might sanctify the people with His own blood, suffered outside the gate.

(Hebrews 13:12)

Jesus Christ did not die in secret or observed by a few people. He was carrying the sin of many. So, many had to see Him when He was crucified. His blood was poured on the ground to sanctify every human walking upon the planet Earth. Once and for all. The death of Christ did not only make an impact in this world but also in other unseen realms.

Mind of Anti-Christ

Anyone who is against Christianity, Christ, the Bible, and the Word of God is an anti-Christ. Well, we all know that the one who is to come is who is the embodiment of Satan Himself.

For as he thinks in his heart, so is he. —PROVERBS 23: 7

You are the way you think. The mind has always been a favorite target of the enemy. If the devil can control your mind, he can control your life. Spirits that attack the mind include mind control, confusion, mental breakdown, mind-binding and mind-binding spirits, insanity, madness, mania, fantasy, evil thinking, migraines, mental pain, and negative thinking. They are all what I call "stinking thinking."

The good news is that you can loose yourself (including your mind) from all evil influences that operate through your mind. Mind control is a common spirit that has been identified by the name "Octopus."

Mind-control spirits can resemble an octopus or squid with tentacles that grasp and control the mind. Deliverance from mind control releases a person from mental pressure, mental pain, confusion, and mental torment. Mind-control spirits can enter through listening to ungodly music, reading occult books, pornography, false teachings, false religions, drugs, and passivity.

In Jesus's name, I loose my mind from all spirits of control, confusion, mental bondage, insanity, madness, fantasy, passivity, intellectualism, knowledge block, ignorance, mind-binding, lust, and evil thinking. Amen.

7 Weapons of God against Mind Control

Word of God
Take the helmet of salvation and the sword of the Spirit, which is the word of God. Ephesians 6:17

For the word of God is living and active. Sharper than any double-edged sword, it penetrates even to dividing soul and spirit, joints and marrow; it judges the thoughts and attitudes of the heart.

Hebrews 4:12

When you are dealing with mental matters, you are dealing with spiritual forces that press you down so you never fully function to your proportion. The enemy wants to confuse you and wants you to walk in darkness. yet it is the Lord who enlightens our darkness. Many should be taught that the enemy is after the mind. The mind is where all things start, doubts, confusion, division, etc.

As someone who has struggled for more than 2 years with mental issues, the Word of God has helped a lot along the journey. The Lord appeared to me at one point and told me that I must not only study the Word but become the Word. As you study the Word, your reflection will change and resemble Christ Himself. All men and women ought to have the mind of Christ.

You can receive salvation for your soul but you also have to receive it through the renewal of your mind. It is the duty of the Holy Spirit to transform our inner man but you cannot relax and allow all sorts of evil thinking to dominate your mind. Think positive. Think purity. Think about what glorifies the Spirit of God.

The Word that is sharper than any two-edged sword shall deliver you from all the wiles of the enemy after your mind.

Prayer

And pray in the Spirit on all occasions with all kinds of prayers and requests. With this in mind, be alert and always keep on praying for all the saints. Eph 6:18 1.

Prayer is the direct engagement of the enemy in spiritual warfare, as we are guided by the Spirit to apply God's Word to spiritual strongholds. Prayer is one of the greatest weapons against the forces of darkness. When you pray more, more trouble comes. Many are surprised when they are so dedicated to prayer and find themselves in deep trouble the more they pray.

I have realized that evil altars that have long been in place are threatened the more we pray. There are different kinds of prayer but in all, heartfelt prayers are destructive bombs. God listens to heartfelt prayers.

As we are dealing with the battle of the mind, warfare prayers are your go-to. I have started with the Word which when you meditate, you are transformed and breaks the strongholds of the mind.

The Word of God and prayer bring forth the light in all our understanding. The light of God silences all the powers of evil. The kingdom of God is the kingdom of light against the kingdom of darkness.

Spirit of heaviness, octopus spirits, and all kinds of depressive spirit takes warfare prayer to be destroyed.

Praying in the Spirit includes all kinds of prayers And pray in the Spirit on all occasions with all kinds of prayers and requests.

With this in mind, be alert and always keep on praying for all the saints. Ephesians 6:18

. . . .

PRAISE, THANKSGIVING, and worship

In the realm of spiritual warfare, dealing with spiritual attacks and the influence of malevolent forces can be a stressful and difficult ordeal. However, the power of praise, worship, and thanksgiving is a transformative tool that can lead to liberation, freedom from demonic mind control, and ultimate spiritual victory. Let's explore how these practices can liberate the mind and spirit, inspired by stories from the Bible, including the remarkable story of the Apostles Paul and Silas in King Jehoshaphat's prison and faith-filled victory.

1. The story of Apostles Paul and Silas:

One of the most inspiring stories of deliverance through praise is found in the New Testament. In Acts 16, we see Paul and Silas imprisoned in Philippi. They were beaten on the back and shackled. In the midst of their dire circumstances, they chose to praise and worship God. Their joyful and heartfelt anthems echoed across the prison walls, attracting the attention of prisoners and guards.

Then something extraordinary happened: an earthquake shook the prison to its core. The prison doors opened and everyone's chains fell off. The warden believed that the prisoners had escaped and, knowing that his life was in danger, attempted suicide. However, Paul and Silas arrested him, and at that moment the jailer witnessed the transforming power of God's presence. He and his entire family believed in Christ and experienced salvation that night.

This story illustrates that even in the most difficult and oppressive circumstances, praise and worship can bring about divine intervention and liberation. This represents the spiritual principle that God dwells in the praise of His people, leading to supernatural breakthroughs.

2. King Jehoshaphat's victory:

Another powerful illustration of the impact of praise, worship, and thanksgiving can be found in the story of King Jehoshaphat in 2 Chronicles 20. When the king faced a threat of war by a coalition of hostile nations, he responded with prayer, worship, and thanksgiving... Thanksgiving.

Jehoshaphat along with the people of Judah sought God's guidance and expressed his dependence on Him through praise and worship. God's response was swift and miraculous. He asked them not to fear the approaching armies, for the battle was his and not theirs.

The king and his people went into battle with praise and worship, putting the loyalists first. As they began to sing and praise, the Lord caused chaos among the enemy, causing them to turn against each other. The result was victory without Judah raising his weapon. This story demonstrates that praise, worship, and thanksgiving can lead to divine intervention and victory, even in the face of insurmountable difficulties. In the face of spiritual attacks and mind control, turning to God in praise and worship can open the path to liberation and freedom.

3. Personal profile:

In our lives, when we face spiritual attacks and demonic influences, we can find inspiration from these biblical examples. Praise, worship, and thanksgiving become our spiritual weapons, releasing divine power in the midst of chaos. By lifting our voices and hearts in gratitude and worship, we invite God's presence to transform our circumstances and free us from mind control and oppression. spirit.

Praise breaks the chains of fear and doubt. Worship invites the presence of the Almighty. Thanksgiving shifts our focus from our problems to God's goodness and faithfulness. These practices create an atmosphere where God's power can be demonstrated. In short, the power of praise, worship, and thanksgiving in spiritual warfare cannot be overstated. These practices have the power to break the chains of spiritual oppression, free us from demonic influence, and lead us to victory. From the stories of the Apostles Paul and Silas

Corporate Life in the Church

Fellowship within a church community is a powerful force that can bring strength and support during spiritual trials and personal difficulties. When you are going through difficult times, especially if you are mentally unstable, the love and support of fellow believers can make all the difference. Here's why it's important:

Solidarity and solidarity:

When believers come together, they form a united front. The collective strength of your church community can help you stay strong against spiritual attacks. Together, you can tackle challenges that seem insurmountable alone. Friendship:

Loneliness and isolation can make mental instability worse. Being part of a church family means you have friends who truly care about your well-being. Their presence can bring comfort and peace of mind.

Prayer Support:

Your church family can lift you up in prayer. When faced with spiritual attacks or mental difficulties, their prayers can be a source of comfort and strength. Knowing that others are praying for you can give you hope and encouragement.

Encouragement:

During difficult times, having people who believe in and encourage you is invaluable. Other believers can inspire you to keep moving forward, reminding you of your value in God's eyes.

Knowledge:

Many members of the Church have faced their own trials and sufferings. They can understand your difficulties, give you a listening ear and a shoulder to lean on. This understanding can help reduce feelings of isolation.

Responsibility:

Church fellowship can provide an organized and supportive environment. When you are struggling, your church community can help you stay on track with your faith and values.

Advice:

Pastors, leaders, and experienced church members can offer spiritual guidance and advice. They can help you deal with spiritual attacks and mental instability, providing wisdom and guidance based on their faith and experience. In short, the strength of collective life in the Church is the strength that comes from community bonds. When you are mentally unstable or facing spiritual challenges, the support, love, and prayers of fellow believers can be a lifesaver. Remember that you are not alone and your church community is here to help you through difficult times.

Tearing down stronghold

In the spiritual realm, the concept of spiritual fortresses is an important battlefield. These strongholds are places where our thoughts and beliefs are held captive by negative and destructive forces, including mind-controlling spirits and evil influences that harm our lives and our health. The Bible, in II Corinthians 10: 3-5, offers helpful advice on how to combat these strongholds, emphasizing that our weapons are not carnal but have the spiritual power to destroy these spiritual strongholds.

The Bible itself provides the roadmap for tearing down these strongholds and regaining spiritual freedom. Let's look at this process and understand the power it holds.

• • • •

1. ACKNOWLEDGE THE existence of strongholds:

The first step to tearing down mental fortresses is to recognize their presence. These strongholds can manifest as recurring negative thought patterns, doubts, fears, or destructive beliefs that hinder personal and spiritual growth.

2. Spiritual warfare:

The Bible makes it clear that the fight against strongholds is not physical but spiritual. It emphasizes the importance of relying on God's divine power. Engaging in prayer, meditation, and spiritual practices can strengthen your connection with God and empower you to fight these spiritual battles.

3. Crush the imagination:

To gain freedom from mind-controlling spirits and evil forces, it is necessary to confront and eliminate negative fantasies and thought patterns that oppose the knowledge of God. This involves actively challenging and rejecting thoughts that conflict with your faith and spiritual understanding. 4. Obedience to Christ:

The ultimate goal of tearing down strongholds is to submit every thought to the obedience of Christ. This means aligning your thoughts and beliefs with the teachings and values of Christ. In doing so, you will gain mental clarity and a strong foundation for your mental and emotional health.

5. Freedom from mind control:

Mind-controlling spirits and evil forces thrive on manipulating and influencing your thoughts. By actively resisting these influences and breaking them through prayer and spiritual development, you can regain control of your mind. This process is transformative, freeing you from the mental chains that hold you captive.

· · · ·

6. BUILD A SOLID SPIRITUAL foundation:

To maintain a stronghold, it is important to build a strong spiritual foundation. This includes regularly reading and meditating on God's Word, participating in a supportive faith community, and seeking guidance from spiritual leaders. A solid foundation helps fortify your mind against future attacks.

Breaking down the stronghold of the mind is a journey of spiritual growth and self-discovery. This is not a one-time event but an ongoing process of renewing your mind and drawing closer to God. Through faith, prayer, and the power of God, you can remove the negative influences that have imprisoned your mind.

By aligning your thoughts and beliefs with the teachings of Christ, you will not only free yourself from mind-controlling evil spirits and forces but also create a resilient and resilient spirit. determined, firmly rooted in faith. In doing so, you experience a transformation in your mind and spirit, paving the way for a more peaceful, joyful, and spiritually fulfilling life. The power to break down strongholds is not only divine but also within your reach, bringing liberation and a renewed mind firmly grounded in the knowledge of God.

Blood of Jesus

"And they overcame him by the blood of the Lamb, and by the word of their testimony." –Revelation 12:11 (KJV)

What can watch away my sins? Nothing but the blood of Jesus. When you understand the righteousness that comes through the blood of Jesus, you are walking in the highest realm of faith. The blood of Jesus is a mystery. The Devil would not have influenced the people of that time to crucify Jesus Christ if he knew what the blood of Christ would do to the human race.

From the time of Adam to Jesus Christ, the blood played a significant role in cleansing, redeeming, and sanctifying the saints of God. From Genesis to Revelation, the words *the blood* are kept before our eyes—a reminder of its importance and significance to God and to us.

The sacrifices of Abel, Noah, and Isaac, the Passover lamb, and the giving of the Law all came to pass, but "not without blood" (Hebrews 9:7, *NKJV*). The blood symbolizes cleansing and purification—the settling of a matter.

The power of the blood of Jesus has provided everything you need to live a life of victory, including Redemption, fellowship, healing, protection, and authority over the devil.

As Christians, we know about the blood, sing hymns about the blood, and remember it during Communion. But how many of us truly know how deep its power runs, and all that it has provided for us? Even more important—how many of us use it and apply it in our lives every day?

The moment I learned about the application of blood over my life, I saw victory from victory. I have walked into a dimension I have never seen before. It was through the revelation of God after a long time suffering defeat from witches and wizards, that I saw the power of the blood. And what the blood of Christ does in the spirit world when you apply it.

No demon can stand the blood of Jesus. The blood of Jesus is the power of God to redeem us. In the spirit realm, the blood of Jesus is the light of glory. It reveals every hidden thing, be it the works of darkness or the iniquities of men.

Moses was commanded to sanctify the priesthood of Aron through the blood. Matter of fact, everything Aron did revolved around the blood sacrifice. Jesus Christ stands as the high priest of the church. knowing the mystery and the power of the blood, we will be victorious in this life and life to come. The power is in the blood. Sadly, occultists, sorcerers, witches, and wizards understand the concepts of blood more than Christians.

There is a power in the blood. While agents of darkness are busy killing chickens and goats, drinking the blood of humans—let us the church be drunk with the holy spirit and be covered with the blood of the lamb. In the spirit realm, you can eat the body of Christ and drink his blood by faith.

On different accounts and occasions, I have seen tremendous victory by invoking the power of the blood of Christ. I have seen the fall of generational altars fall in my bloodline. I have seen territorial strongholds over my village flee because of the blood. It is vital to pray and apply the blood of the Lamb especially when you are under attack.

Healing Through the Blood of Jesus

"By His stripes, we are healed." –Isaiah 53:5 (NKJV)

When you take Communion, do you think of healing? Most Christians take the emblem of the blood and say, "Thank God, we are delivered from sin," and that is true. Praise God for it!

But according to Isaiah 53:4-5, Jesus' sacrifice covered every area of man's existence. He bore spiritual torment for our sins, mental distress for our worry, care, sorrow, and fear, as well as physical pain for our sickness and disease. The stripes He bore and the blood He shed were for our healing. By His stripes, we are healed.

God gave everything He had to redeem mankind from the curse. When we receive only part of His sacrifice, it's an insult to Him (see this prophecy by Kenneth Copeland). When we apply the blood of Jesus and receive its power, we need to remember to apply it in its fullness. Don't just receive and apply it halfway. Accept everything Jesus' sacrifice provided. If you fail to understand and receive the full power of the blood, you will be missing out.

Paul wrote, "For this cause many are weak and sickly among you, and many sleep" (1 Corinthians 11:30, KJV).

Learn How to Take Communion for Your Healing here.

If you need healing today, the blood of Jesus is free and without side effects. You don't need a prescription, you don't need an appointment, and you don't have to check with your insurance company. Jesus provided it all through the blood! You can appropriate the blood of Jesus for your healing today.

Spiritual Fasting

Patients with nervous and mental disorders, paralysis, semi-paralysis, neurasthenia, and other forms of insanity have been cured through the power of fasting and prayer. Fasting is a critical way of 'house-cleaning' the body and the Holy Spirit will be pleased to dwell in a 'clean temple'.

In most of our lives, we are preoccupied with many things. If it is not breaking news, it's media, music, fashion, or food, all these things make us focus on the moment. While it is not a bad thing to focus on the moment, there is life beyond what we can see with our naked eye.

I always tell people that, if you want to experience the presence of God to the fullest, deny your flesh. We cannot meet with a spiritual God with our flesh. Many matters that affect our minds are spiritual matters. And it is a disaster if you would try to solve spiritual matters carnally. Spiritual things for spiritual things.

Fasting and prayer have been the pillars of the heart of the power of the gospel of Jesus Christ. When men and women seek powers from above, they kneel down and humble themselves before the king.

When you have been practicing prayer and fasting for so long, you will understand that your body turns into fire. You become bold, you pray more and your faith increases when you are fasting. You will also start to appreciate the Word of God more and more. This is what the ancient people used to do.

Apostle Paul was empowered through the power of fasting and prayer. Remember, he spent three days without eating and drinking after his encounter with Christ. He also went on to live a fast lifestyle.

He is the preacher who suffered for the gospel of Jesus Christ more than all Apostles in the bible. You start to have a sense of direction and purpose after prayer and fasting. Not that you do not, it's just that when your spirit you sense more of the spiritual matter and are able to discern spiritual things.

I have written a lot about fasting and prayer. Especially if you are constantly under spiritual attacks and spiritual battle—fasting and prayer will shed light and you will be victorious.

Before humans learned how to farm, people hunted and gathered food to survive. They would go long stretches without eating. It took a lot of energy and time to gather nuts and berries or hunt game. The human body adapted to that by using what stores of energy it had. Today you don't have to hunt and gather your food the way your ancestors did, but fasting may still benefit your physical and mental well-being.

Fasting can benefit you in a few simple ways:

1. Sharper mind:

When you fast, your body has fewer harmful substances in your blood and lymphatic system. This allows you to think more easily because the energy normally used to digest food is made available to your brain. It can take a few days for this mental boost to take effect and you may initially feel a headache or irritability. But once your body eliminates toxins, your brain functions better and you have clearer thoughts, improved memory, and heightened senses.

2. Treatment:

Fasting helps your body rejuvenate by eliminating unhealthy cells and preserving healthy cells. It also moves essential nutrients through your body. It retains vitamins and minerals while removing old tissues, toxins, and unwanted elements.

3. Add will:

Fasting is a difficult choice that requires mental strength and the ability to resist immediate rewards for long-term benefits. When you successfully complete your fast, you will feel very satisfied and accomplished.

. . . .

SPIRITUAL WARFARE PRAYERS

Prayer Points:

1. Blood of Jesus saturate and cleans my mind, in the name of Jesus.
2. Every stronghold of the mind in my life, scatter by fire, in the name of Jesus.
3. Internal battle, terminate now, in the name of Jesus.
4. Evil thought, tormenting me, dry up to your root, in the name of Jesus.
5. I silence every lie of the devil in my mind, in the name of Jesus.
6. Evil voice speaking to my mind, be silence and die, in the name of Jesus.
7. Witchcraft imagination in my life, scatter, in the name of Jesus.
8. Witchcraft plantation, come out with all your roots, in the name of Jesus.
9. Every battle of the mind, assigned to kill me, terminate and die, in the name of Jesus.
10. Depression in my life, die now, in the name of Jesus.
11. Every problem that entered into my life through my mind, die, in the name of Jesus.
12. Powers dominating and controlling me from my mind, be roasted by fire now, in the name of Jesus.
13. My mind, receive power for productivity, in the name of Jesus.

Notes

Https://www.rhemabiblechurch.net/index.php/articles/prayers/1172-shake-yourself-free-from-mental-attacks[1]

https://emilyroselewis.org/2018/03/24/the-octopus-spirit/

https://www.faithwalkapostolicministries.com/single-post/2019/09/06/the-demonic-spirit-octopus

https://blog.kcm.org/power-blood-jesus/

ECCLESIA CHURCH OF GOD IN CHRIST, Pastor Luther H. Holmes, Jr. March 17, 2021

Bible Study Series, The Reality of Spiritual Warfare.

Winning The Mindwars: Tearing Down Strongholds Through Prayer by Steve Berger

---

1. https://www.rhemabiblechurch.net/index.php/articles/prayers/1172-shake-yourself-free-from-mental-attacks

Don't miss out!

Visit the website below and you can sign up to receive emails whenever Johannes Tefo publishes a new book. There's no charge and no obligation.

https://books2read.com/r/B-A-UEZX-JQNYC

Did you love *Deliverance From Mind Control: Be Free And Delivered From Every Marine Demons Of Mind Control*? Then you should read *Identity In Christ*[2] by Johannes Tefo!

IDENTITY IN CHRIST

JOHANNES TEFO

3

Uncover who you truly are in Christ with "Identity in Christ"! This book helps you see yourself differently, with stories and easy-to-understand lessons. It's like a guide showing you how loved and special you are to God. You'll learn to be confident and find your purpose, feeling free from doubts and fears. If you're unsure about yourself or want to feel closer to God, this book is for you. Get ready to be inspired and discover the awesome

---

2. https://books2read.com/u/bzry0L

3. https://books2read.com/u/bzry0L

person you were meant to be. Dive into "Identity in Christ" now and start your journey to feeling whole and loved!

Also by Johannes Tefo

Family spiritual Warfare Books
Youth's Guide To Spiritual Warfare
A Women's Guide To Spiritual Warfare

Standalone
Deliver Your Soul From Evil
Overcoming Spirit Of Stagnation
The 24: Prophetic Word For This Season 2024 And Beyond
Michael For Warfare
Territorial Spirits: Overcome Evil Strongholds in Your Life And
Take Over Your Community With Strategic Warfare And
Winning Prayers
Prayers Against Suicide Spirit
Spiritual Warfare When Enough is Enough
Identity In Christ
Prayers Against Satanic Networks
The Workplace You Need: Spiritual Warfare Prayers That
Silence Evil Powers At Your Workplace.

Deliverance From Mind Control: Be Free And Delivered From Every Marine Demons Of Mind Control

About the Author

Before he started writing Christian books, Johannes got a graduate degree in Film and Television from university of Johannesburg. After that, just to shake things up, he went to equip himself with religious studies, particularly Christianity, just to have knack about the world beyond the curtains of time. And how this body of Christ has transformed millions of people around the world, not neglecting how sadly the movement has been persecuted from time to time. He now writes full time.

www.ingramcontent.com/pod-product-compliance
Lightning Source LLC
Chambersburg PA
CBHW070919160726
48004CB00003B/1435